Kit Calvert
Yorkshire Dalesman

In this series:
THE FABULOUS CLIFFORDS
REGINALD FARRER
DALESFOLK & DIALECT

Kit Calvert

Yorkshire Dalesman

W R MITCHELL

CASTLEBERG
2003

A **Castleberg** Book

First published in the United Kingdom in 2003

Copyright © W R Mitchell 2003

The moral right of the author has been asserted

ISBN 1 871064 38 4

Typeset in Giovanni, printed and bound in the
United Kingdom by Lamberts Printers,
Station Road, Settle, North Yorkshire, BD24 9AA

Published by Castleberg, 18 Yealand Avenue, Giggleswick,
Settle, North Yorkshire, BD24 0AY

Contents

Illustrations

Cover photograph of Kit Calvert – by courtesy of *The Yorkshire Post*. Cheese label featuring Kit – by courtesy of Wensleydale Creamery, Hawes. Photographs of the interior of the Creamery and of Swaledale – W R Mitchell. Drawings by Fred Lawson, who lived at Castle Bolton in Wensleydale. Art supplement – photos of Kit Calvert in workaday attire; also of his prototype car and funeral – by kind permission of *The Yorkshire Post*. Photo of Kit after his visit to Buckingham Palace – J C Moore. Other photography – W R Mitchell.

INTRODUCTION

I first met Kit in 1948, when I joined Harry Scott at *The Dalesman*. Harry had initiated a "pocket book" series that included *The Story of Wensleydale Cheese*, by T C Calvert, which was Kit's "Sunday name". On the title page was a woodcut, by Marie Hartley, of a farmer hand-milking a cow. When Kit was a lad, milking might take place in some remote pasture so that meadow grass was left untrampled in the weeks before haytime. The milk was transported to the farm in a back-can. Kit told me when old, diehard farmers "salved" their sheep just before tupping time in November. The fleece of a sheep was shed [parted] in strips and a mixture of Russian tar and rancid butter applied to the skin. Salved sheep, it was said, wintered well and were also free of insect pests.

As editor of *The Dalesman* for many years, I became a close friend of Kit, his little dog, Lassie and Dolly the pony. Kit's mind was a repository for dale-country lore. Lolling in a chair before the fireplace, still wearing his floppy trilby, he would draw fumes of black twist up the stem of a clay pipe and, within seconds, relate tales of t'auld days. I heard of the baby born in a great snowstorm who was taken from his mother's arms to the bedroom window and shown what a grim world he had come into. Just before the Great War, Tommy and Jennie Taylor received their first 7s.6d from the State – 5s for the householder and 2s.6d for his wife. "With a pension for life, they thought they were in heaven."

Kit's first crossing of the Buttertubs Pass, between Hardraw in Wensleydale and t'top end of Swaledale, had been in a horse-drawn outfit belonging to Elijah Allen. It was Muker Show day in 1913. The youngest and fittest passengers dismounted and walked up the steep parts. A trip of modest mileage took about two and a-half hours. Said Kit: "For a schoolboy it was the adventure of the year. I felt to be going into another world." During a winter spell in the 1939-45 war, after taking a service at the Congregational chapel in Keld, he found Buttertubs Pass was wrapped in mist. He drove his car with open windows, listening and applying the brakes if a slurring of pebbles indicated he had strayed from the road.

Kit Calvert died in January, 1984. A few days before he "passed away", Kit had returned to me the proof of an article he had written for *The Dalesman* about gezlings [goslings]. With it was a brief note reporting that he was "off colour" but would be much better when the spring weather came. I was delighted at being asked to contribute a piece about him to the *New National Dictionary of Biography*. A normally staid academic acknowledged it with the words: "What a guy!"

EARLY DAYS

Kit's earliest memory was of being awakened by a screeching sound as the horse-drawn quarry lorries, en route for Hawes station, were checked on the descent from Burtersett to the main road. The screeching sound came from a primitive braking system. A wheel rode on a wedge-shaped *slipper* attached by a chain to the frame of the cart. The *slipper* left a rut in the waterbound road. By directing two wagon wheels into the grove, the carter kept a heavy wagon on a straight course, to the annoyance of the county surveyor. The screeching sound began as early as six o' clock, when the first of the quarry wagons, drawn by splendid Shire horses, descended the hill on its way to Hawes railway station. On winter mornings, roused by the quarry sounds, the lads awoke to six-inch shivers and to window panes silvered by frost.

At Burtersett, quarrymen outnumbered farmers. Each cottage bulged with humanity. A cousin of Kit, with a two-up, two-down house, accommodated his wife and twelve children. Elsewhere, lodgers, mainly young men seeking work in the quarries, temporarily augmented the family. On Quarry Hill, two commercial enterprises operated. Each was owned by a member of the large Metcalfe clan. Richard Metcalfe was known as Old Dicky Bokiter. His competitor was Tom Metcalfe. Between them they employed about eighty men. The main products were flags cut to order for the expanding textile towns of Lancashire. Kit's father, John Edward Calvert, nicknamed Moss, devoted himself for a year to producing square slabs with circular holes to accommodate manhole covers for London.

Thomas Christopher Calvert – our Kit – was born at Burtersett on April 26, 1903, being the eldest of the three sons of Moss Calvert and his wife Rose (nee Fothergill). Kit's nickname was Moss-Kit. The Calverts lived in straitened times. Grandfather Calvert, a long-time quarryman, was so impoverished he ended his working life with the hard, tedious task of breaking stones so they were of a size suitable for repairing the roads. He who earned less than £1 a week for six days in the quarry received 1s.10d for every cubic yard of broken stone he produced. This meant he was paid less than 2s for eight hours of hard graft.

The quarry owners recruited strong young men, worked them unremittingly and eventually cast them off without a penny in compensation. Kit's father, one of an over-stressed labour force, worked for ten hours a day, six days a week for eighteen years. With deductions, including the rent of his house, he was paid 16s.2d. He had but one week's holiday – his honeymoon in 1902 – and the only regular holidays were on Good Friday and Christmas Day.

At Burtersett, the best stone came from drifts that penetrated the hillside for anything up to half a mile. Underground workers were said to be "up t'hole". The levels had exotic names, including Peacock, Fancy End and Red Gate. Pillars of rock were left so that the roof was supported. As no explosives could be used, the men were provided with hand-drills. Young Kit standing in the dressing-shed, saw slabs of sandstone being deftly trimmed into paving flags or roofing slates. The men worked outdoors in summer. Boys with barrows moved chippings to the spoil-heaps. A ringing sound emanated from a blacksmith's shop where blunt picks were sharpened.

The subterranean world was aglow with the light of tallow candles, purchased – a hundredweight at a time – from Candle Willie of Hawes, who was yet another Metcalfe. Willie rendered down mutton or beef fat in a container over a fire. The wicks, draped from a wheel-like structure, were gently lowered into the fat. As they were drawn out, some of the fat adhered to the wicks. The size of a candle was determined by the number of times a wick was dipped in the cauldron.

BOYHOOD

Kit grew up in a stone cottage. The bareness of the flagged ground floor was partly concealed by "pegged" rugs, formed of multi-coloured strips from old clothing with a backing of hessian. The kitchen range, supplied by Bowerbank, ironmongers of Penrith, was given a weekly application of black-lead. An oven and a boiler that was a major source of hot water, flanked the fireplace. A large kettle usually had a song in its heart. Overall, the cottage was damp and a playground for eager draughts.

Many local families augmented their income by keeping geese and hens. A good goose was said to lay on Candlemas Day. Nesting facilities for Moss Calvert's geese were tea chests lagged with clean hay and situated in the back kitchen. Money from the sale of goslings went towards new clothes for the children. One year, when the gander proved to be infertile, and no eggs hatched, the Calvert boys had the indignity of wearing last year's clothes at chapel for the Sunday

School Anniversary.

By August or September, the goslings were not easily distinguished from their parents. Time was when Frank Clapham of Askrigg bought up surplus young geese, collecting them at a small paddock adjoining Penny Garth in Hawes. Before driving them by road to arable land between Ripon and York they were coaxed through a shallow pool of warm tar, then through fine sand, which adhered to the tar, reinforcing the webbed feet of the birds against the rough road. Subsequently, a Keighley man, who advertised himself as The Gosling King, bought geese at Hawes on market day and transported them to his home town by rail.

Hens belonging to Kit's family spent much of the year in a hut erected in the corner of a meadow. The hens were transferred to an outpasture from May until the end of haytime. It was a daily chore for Kit and Bob, in turn, to feed the hens and collect any eggs. In good times, the eggs sold at sixteen for a shilling. If the price dropped, Kit's mother preserved the eggs in water-glass, setting them aside for use on baking days in winter.

If eggs were served, father had a whole egg and Kit

and his brother Bob shared at another. When Kit requested an egg for himself, his mother remarked that half an egg had been good enough when Lloyd George was being raised, "so it's good enough for thee". The Calverts ate what they could catch. On a Saturday evening, young Kit was despatched to the butcher for a sheep's head, with eyes, price thruppence. By removing the eyes and skinning the head himself, Kit saved the family a penny. The sheep-head was boiled in an iron pan suspended from a reckon over the open fire.

Owd Mary, Kit's grandmother, lived austerely. One day, she told Ann, her eldest daughter to "put t-fire to t'oven" while she went to Billy Willie's [the grocer] for "a few bits o' things to bake wi'." Grandmother set off with a half crown in her purse, which was the only money she possessed. En route, she called to see the Jacksons, who lived in even more straitened circumstances, and found the emaciated old couple lying in bed. Grannie used her half a crown to buy food for the Jacksons. The cost being 4s.6d, the grocer marked 2s "on the slate." He was untroubled when Grannie mentioned who would be receiving the food. She refused to pay the two shillings and as far as Kit knew she never settled that account. "There were many in Burtersett who would have paid it if they had known. For many of us were in debt to Owd Mary."

Kit and brother Bob began attending Hawes Council School after the Easter holidays in 1908, having a round trip of three miles a day. They wore clogs that had iron caulkers and carried their mid-day food in satchels. Theirs was a recurring diet of jam sandwiches, plus half a bannock speckled with currants. Each Tuesday, Kit received a halfpenny as spending money, visiting a shop in Hawes owned by Old Tommy Metcalfe, who was known to one and all as Tommy Spiffs. Mrs Metcalfe stood waiting, alongside boxes of sweets. "We rooted among them." She put them in cones she made from pages of the church magazine.

Kit was still attending school in 1913 when his father resigned from his work in the quarry. He had asked the owner to increase his wage from eighteen to twenty shillings. This was refused. So the Calvert family lost their income and also their "tied" home. When the Great War was raging and most young men were in the Forces, father found work as a yardman at Hawes auction mart. With the job came a substantial house.

HAWES

Hawes, sixteen miles from the nearest towns – from Sedbergh, Kirkby Stephen, Ingleton and Leyburn – was a community in which isolation had bred self-reliance and a deep pride in belonging. Viewed from the Widdale road, the place had an open-ended appearance. You looked directly into the heart of the town and half-expected to see hitching-posts for horses. When Kit was young, Hawes languished in a changing world. The world may be dropping to bits but the folk of Hawes managed to stay pretty much as they were.

Livestock were no longer displayed, messily, in the main street, where a handclasp sealed a bargain. Transactions were now being undertaken at the auction mart. To the horse fair, on September 28, were driven ponies raised on the fells. These lively animals were unbroken, unshod, most of them destined to be bought for shaft work in the industrialised towns of the north-east. John Oswald Dinsdale, who shod many of the ponies, reckoned that when he had finished the job, an animal was as good as broken in for work. Motor vehicles were such a novelty that when John, startled by one, fell to the ground, the driver insisted he must receive compensation. Said a still bewildered John: "What do you usually pay?"

My first chat with Kit Calvert took place in 1948 on the bridge that spans Duerley Beck. Kit's blue eyes twinkled under a mop of hair that in turn was capped by a floppy brown trilby. Kit held a clay pipe in a mouth clenched as tightly as a vice. He was thus able to kindle the pipe single-handedly. His dog, lying flat out, like a grey-brown door-mat, had its eyes closed. We did not feel to be in any danger. Cars passed at the rate of one every ten minutes. More than one driver stopped and wound down a window to join in the conversation. The Hawes in which Kit had grown up, forty years before, was a farmer's town in which nicknames proliferated – Funny, Falk, Stump Aat, Cracken Peg, Bella Jack, and many more. Happily, he was not destined to follow the family trade of quarryman. With changes in materials used for building, no market remained for hand-dressed flags and slate.

At Work

At the age of ten, Kit worked at a boarding house in Hawes on Saturday. He earned fourpence – and was provided with a good lunch. Subsequently, he was in farm service at Lowgate, not far from home, working for Ralph Waggett. His boss, a good Methodist, had been a lead-miner in Swaledale, as was testified by his dry cough, a hint of the dreaded gruver's disease, a form of silicosis. Completing the Waggett household were a wife and an unmarried daughter called Alice. Food was adequate and well-cooked. One meal included a curious red fruit. Kit was tasting his first tomato.

Initially, he was paid five shillings a week, plus full board and lodging. Work included a daily task of carrying milk in a seven-gallon back-can from field to house. If more than seven gallons was produced, he was allowed to use the donkey and side-cans. The donkey was stubborn. It was partial to tobacco. When it became awkward and refused to move, Kit fed it plugs of black twist. (An ounce of twist cost him thruppence halfpenny). Kit himself became addicted to tobacco. He chewed it for a year or two before smoking it in a clay pipe – the sort used by the old-time lead-miners of the northern dales.

Kit stayed with the Waggetts for two and a-half years, during which time his weekly wage rose to seven shillings. That was all the old chap could afford. Kit then stood the hirings at Hawes, hoping to be discovered by someone who would employ him for ten shillings a week. It was at the hirings, held twice a year, that farm labourers and servant girls renewed their contracts or offered their services to new masters or mistresses.

In the years before the Great War, Irishmen seeking haytime employment – a month's work, at a specified wage, board and lodgings included – attended a hiring fair at Hawes. They travelled by train up the Long Drag to Garsdale, where they changed to the Hawes train. Nervous people locked their houses. On the morning of the second Tuesday in July, knots of Irishmen presented themselves to be hired. Kit, who was never hired in this way, was to recall the Irish invasion, and the hiring fair at which "t'awd farmers waddled along wi' their walking sticks. As they passed the Irishmen, they'd look at 'em as though they were kenning sheep in a pen at the auction mart."

Kit, aged fifteen, was standing the hirings for the first time. He had almost given up hope of a job when Moses Atkinson, a cattle-dealer from Bainbridge, espied him. (Moses, who stood out in a crowd because he wore a billycock and carried a bamboo stick, had prospered during the heady days prior to the Great War and would lose all his money in the post-War economic crash). To Kit's astonishment, he was offered the handsome sum of £1 a week. At Moses' farm, a housekeeper prepared the food. Kit was at hand when his boss wished to travel by horse and trap. He dare not take the reins himself, being more often drunk than sober.

Kit had his introduction to the chancy world of cattle-dealing and, by watching a cow-doctor named Dick Bell, into the diagnosis and cures of bovine ailments. Moses showed him how to make an average cow look superb at the auction mart by waxing its horns and adding rouge to the "bag". Kit invested the money he earned in young stock, both lambs and calves. Kit's next employer, James Scarr, lived at the imposing Colby Hall, Askrigg, where there was a big herd of Shorthorn cattle and innumerable sheep that grazed Abbotside Common. On winter evenings, James carved walking sticks, using hazel shoots plucked from hedge or woodland. During the five years Kit worked for the Scarr family, he went "from lad to man."

In 1924, Kit's life took a new turn following a serious accident. He was travelling pillion on a motor cycle being driven by a friend. They were on their way to a dance. Having rounded a bend, the driver of the bike swerved to avoid a horse and milk-float in charge of a drunken farmer. Kit's right leg struck the iron hub of a cart wheel and was shattered. He was knocked unconscious. The limb was so badly damaged Kit spent two and a-half months in Leeds Infirmary while doctors painstakingly re-assembled it. Kit had plenty of time to reflect on the accident and on the fact that the farmer in the milk-float had not bothered to stop.

THE DALESMAN'S COW

The morning milk-run from the farms to Hawes station was a spectacle not without interest. Kit recalled that the farmers and their horse-drawn milk floats were usually in a hurry. They must not miss putting the big milk kits on the early train. "You'd hear 'em coming up. I watched a chap turn in at t'station gates just as train arrived. Another farmer was coming out, with empty churns. Bang! What a mess!" Much of the milk produced in the upper dale was bought by big dealers in Manchester, Leeds, even Newcastle and ultimately by a succession of big companies.

Kit could not discover the period when the Shorthorn first took the place of the Wensleydale ewe as the farmers' milk producer. A reasonable guess would place the change somewhere between the dissolution of the monasteries and the seventeenth century. "By the mid-17th century the sheep were being farmed for the value of their wool and mutton while the cow was considered to be the milk-producing animal."

Well within Kit's farming experience the Shorthorn breed of cow languished in the flower-decked fields of the dale-country. Stock was over-wintered in many coo-houses, from six to twelve young stock being accommodated in each. The cows were tied lightly by the neck, being turned out daily to drink at a handy spring. "In a bad winter there was plenty of snow for 'em to lick at. Snow blew in through cracks in the roof or around the doors."

From November to May, the Shorthorns subsisted on hay laboriously cut by knife from the "mew" that extended from the main floor of the building to cob-web-festooned beams. An autumn-calver might be left indoors as early as October. Turning Out Day for milkers was May 20, if the weather was settled. (Young cattle would have been put out "mebbe a week 'afore"). An old chap known to Kit, being a stickler for tradition, let his milk cows out on May 20 even if they were being bombarded by hailstones. Kit's inclination, if the weather was good and "there was a bit o' bite for 'em," was to let them out a week earlier.

The Shorthorn, a thrifty beast, made few demands on a farm's resources and was a dual-purpose breed, yielding good quality milk or beef. This animal, which was red, white or a blend known as "roan", carried its age well. With its horns nicely turned up, it looked sprightly and young. The average Dairy Shorthorn, which "wasn't pushed wi' concentrates", would give you a butter-fat content of about 3.7, some even more, if they weren't making a big lot o'milk. Kit used to test the milk produced in the herd of a farmer who was one of the leaders of introducing Friesian cattle below Leyburn. "We had a celebration if his milk got above 3.1." Shorthorn milk had a high percentage of butter-fat and was ideal for making butter or cheese. "When you'd poured milk into bowls, and left it, to separate the cream, you knew it was ready when the cream would 'od a penny."

Old Shorthorns nivver seemed to die, said Kit. "They were usually sold to someone just before they expired!" Many young in-calf cows were bought by the cow-keepers of Liverpool. They were closely related to families living in the upper dales. Cattle intended for Liverpool must look as though they'd give a canny drop o' milk with good artificial feeding.

Attending to ailing cows was a chancy matter. Many farmers put their faith in a concoction known as "black bottle". Linseed oil and castor oil were frequently used to cure a "stoppage". Engine oil and black sulphur were applied to ringworm. Kit told me of one farmer who used collop [bacon] fat and brimstone – wi' a bit o' turpentine. "Mixed up well, it was claimed never to fail."

Jack Harrison, a Methodist local preacher – "a popular and decent man" – bought a cow which on further examination was found to have a "knot in her tit", a natural swelling forming a hard pellet. It did not stop the milk-flow but made milking that teat slow and awkward. Two years later, a local farmer bought a cow from Jack and later complained bitterly about a "knot" in a teat. He didn't think a Methody preacher would sell a defective animal. Jack replied: "I thowt thou knew all about it. Thou selt yon cow to me!"

A bull was never trusted. In August, a particularly dangerous month, an animal was inclined to "mak a terrible noise and mak' sods fly." Because some farmers were not particular about the type of bull they used, the Shorthorn stock declined in quality. With an increased milk demand, the Dales Shorthorn got a "smittlin'" of other breeds such as the Ayrshire.

THE SLUMP

B ack at Hawes, in the late 1920s, Kit was an odd job man at the auction mart, where in about 1912 he had built a boundary wall, being paid eighteen shillings a rood [seven yards] for the work. He left the employ of the mart when his request for a wage increase from 18s to £1 was refused. Kit asserted his independence. He bought cattle, on commission, for a dealer. He rented two fields, totalling five acres, and a barn, just big enough to house four cows. He became friendly with an ailing farmer at Hawes who, when he died 1931, was found to have remembered Kit's help in his will, leaving him the residue of his estate – almost £300. Kit managed to rent the farm for £70 a year. The man's housekeeper, who had inherited the house, allowed Kit to sell milk in the kitchen. Customers arrived with jugs. Kit took surplus milk to the nearby creamery.

Kit married Jennie Horn, a daleswoman. The housekeeper having died, Kit bought the house – and continued to sell his milk through the kitchen. In his first year of farming, against a backdrop of industrial depression, he received fivepence a gallon for milk in summer and eightpence in winter. He broke with tradition when he bought an Ayrshire cow for £19.10s because she was a good milker, giving six gallons a day. (At calving time she was prone to develop milk fever, alleviated by pumping air into her teats with a bicycle pump. After four years, Kit sold her on).

Kit's top lambs made £2 each. A year later, the price had fallen to 30s. It dropped further, to 17s.3d, before conditions began to improve. He arranged with a destitute farmer to slaughter lambs, one at a time, so the meat might be hawked in a basket. Anything the hapless man made over 16s a lamb would be split between them.

Twice a year, on rent day, the tenant farmers faced the fact they had little or no ready cash. Benny Taylor, agent for the Metcalfes of Ings House estate, met the tenants in the *Crown Hotel*. The first farmer would moan; he could not pay the rent. The next, of more jovial disposition, agreed to send Benny some "brass" when he'd "selled" a cow. An optimist like Jack Chapman remarked: "Well, there's nowt this quarter,

Benny. I've nowt. You've nowt. So there's nowt for noan of us. I'll pull a bit of old fence down and put up a new stretch – and we'll call it a day." Life in the towns was even more desperate than it was in the country. Kit, driving through colliery villages in the North East, saw boarded up shops and men, pinched, starved and grey, sitting or crouching round a war memorial.

He travelled over the Buttertubs Pass into Swaledale to buy up bankrupt stock. Some ewes cost him 5s.6d each. He bought the old tup for 7s.6d, also hens at 9d each, with a small hen hut "thrown in". Two lads who assisted Kit to drive the stock back to Wensleydale were delighted when he gave them the hens and the hut.

Kit weathered the economic storm mainly because a year before he moved to Hawes he met Professor Holman, a full-time lecturer for the Workers' Educational Association, who was seeking to establish classes in the northern dales. Kit was invited to establish more classes in and around Hawes. He inaugurated three and received a regular income of £2.5s a week.

Above: Old-time Hawes on market day.
Below: Sheep sale at the auction mart, where both Kit and his father found employment.

Left: Testing Wensleydale cheese at Hawes Creamery.

Right: John Mason, retired railwayman, who assisted Kit Calvert in his bookshop.

Kit Calvert, complete with clay pipe. Kit first bought tobacco to placate a stubborn donkey. When he began to smoke he resorted to the type of clay pipe favoured by the old-time lead-miners of the dale-country. Never one to impress, he remained "Kit" to everyone he met.

Kit, with a briar in his mouth. The setting is Hawes, where he went to school. In his later life, Kit made a playground for the children of the town. In this photograph, he was standing in the main street, not far from the single-room bookshop that bore his name.

Kit attempted to break into the mass car market with his Curlew two-stroke front-wheel-drive car. Having engine design faults and clocking up only twenty-five miles, it was written off in 1947 and subsequently sold for £250 at a sale held in Middleham in 1984.

Kit Calvert, MBE. He was honoured during the Queen's Jubilee and received his medal from the Queen Mother in February, 1977.

Kit once remarked: "If I leave Hawes, it will be in a box." And so it was in January, 1984. By his own request, his coffin was hauled to the graveside on a cart drawn by Dolly, his old pony. During the journey, the cart was flanked by some of his many dale-country friends.

CHEESE-MAKER

When Kit Calvert was a lad, hardly any of the milk left the farms as milk. It was converted into butter, which was sold or bartered for groceries and other essentials. At small-holdings in Wensleydale and Swaledale, cheese was a speciality. It had been so since monastic times. The monks who settled at Jervaulx and other places in the Dales locked up some of the spring and summer protein in cheese; it could be consumed in leaner times.

The milk they used came from sheep. Kit wrote: "We stand in reverence and awe as we gaze at the ruins of Fountains or Jervaulx but the true and lasting memorial is not in the stately ruins but in the miles and miles of limestone walls and that delicacy, a ripe blue-veined Wensleydale cheese." The monks milked the ewes twice daily. "The Shorthorn cow superseded sheep for the production of milk but the process of cheese-making has been handed down with slight alterations from mother to daughter since those

Flemish holy men lived contentedly in the shadow of our hills."

The name Wensleydale cheese is generic, used for dale-country cheese. At one time, farmhouse cheese was pickled – salted in brine. Kit observed that "a well-made, fully cured pickled cheese was considered to be the finest flavoured Wensleydale cheese obtainable." Wensleydale had a nutty flavour that came from the moisture content. It more or less melted in the mouth. "To me," said Kit, "there was nothing like a good summer-made white Wensleydale cheese."

Much inferior was the "whangby" cheese, made by "greedy folk" of blue [skimmed] milk or half-skim milk. The cheese did not get the correct percentage of butterfat and was hard, fit for nothing but cooking and being usually sold at a much lower price than the full-cream cheese. Rennet, which was used to "lift the curd", was bought from a druggist in Hawes, though "lang since" the dalesfolk used keslop, which came from the stomach of a calf.

The state of the soil and the "herb of the land" were prime factors in making good cheese. The night's milk was poured into a copper cheese-kettle that was kept by t'firespot and left overnight for the souring process to take place. Marjorie Longstaff, one of those who kept the tradition of farmhouse cheese-making alive until the mid-1980s, farmed Deer Park, Harkerside, high above the river Swale. The milk came from Tiny, an eight-year-old red Shorthorn cow with a crumpled horn and Blackie, a matronly Friesian. Marjorie had absorbed her knowledge simply by watching her mother stirring in the rennet, separating curds from whey and packing the curds into tin vats to be placed in a cheese press. It had been a common sight until the creation of the Milk Marketing Board in the 1930s.

A June cheese was good for eating about October. A month-old cheese was not considered fit to be cut. It was a bit too "curdy" and needed time to break down. It would be ready to be eaten in about eight weeks and retained its quality for another twelve weeks. The old blue cheese, as made at Carr End, was a favourite of Penry Williams, MP for Middlesbrough, who called at the farm in summer to order the cheese he wanted. This would be collected in the following summer. Penry ate his cheese at Christmas, when it was eighteen months old.

Kit Calvert had watched Aunt Nanny make crumbly Wensleydale and, given a hunk of cheese, he would let it linger in his mouth before swallowing it. Nanny used the morning milk for cheese-making (the afternoon milk was converted into butter). He became an authority on the factory production of Wensleydale cheese. In 1897, Edward Chapman, of Hawes, whose normal business was corn and provisions, had been dissatisfied by some of the farmhouse cheese that was offered to him. He bought a former woollen mill and went into production using local milk. At first, his daily intake was about 200 gallons. He rejoiced in being able to control the quality of cheese, acknowledging that faulty cheese deteriorates rapidly, whereas a first-class cheese, like good port, improves with age. (At about the same time, Alfred Rowntree opened creameries at Masham, then in Coverdale).

In the 1930s, the Hawes creamery, now owned by Captain Goodwin, suffered as the demand for its cheese fell away. By the early part of 1933, the owner could not pay his debts and advised Kit and other suppliers of milk to render him bankrupt. With a threat of closure, a group of six creditors – including Ed Preston, the previous owner, an emissary of

Express Dairy Company and Kit – took over management of the dairy and sold the cheese. It was arranged that when sufficient money had been made to meet the debts, the business would be returned to the owner.

Six months later, when the position was reviewed, they were at least £200 worse off than when they started. Work continued until October, when the Milk Marketing Board was established. The Hawes men took advantage of the rise in demand for cheese prior to Christmas, after which things went dead. The management committee was wound up, each creditor receiving 12s in the £ plus a sixteen pound Wensleydale cheese for every £ of debt. Kit was amused when a testy old farmer who was about to draw £43.4s and no less than seventy-two cheeses asked to be given £40, adding they might keep t'bloody cheeses, which was "more than I expected to git." The remaining £60 – and the company – were handed back to Captain Goodwin. Kit happily returned to his first love, farming.

Within a year, Goodwin was in trouble, this time over money owed to the Milk Marketing Board. The Board foreclosed on him. Kit called a meeting at

Hawes Town Hall. The dalesmen were persuaded – reticently, after much hard talking – to form their own company with a capital of £1,085. Kit, who had put £200 in the scheme, became the secretary and manager. He worked for the first year without pay and was subsequently paid £4 a week. He travelled to London to meet officials of the Marketing Board; they demanded a deposit of £500 – about half his capital – as security. He then had to pay £800 for the creamery and managed to obtain a mortgage of £650.

Kit re-started the business with £435 in the bank and the urgent need to buy vats, shelves and a Ford truck to collect the milk. Arrangements were made to process 500 gallons of milk a day. Wensleydale Dairy Products, Ltd., went into production with a board of nine directors and a cheesemaker at 35s a week. An assistant cheesemaker was paid 25s a week. A lad was recruited as general help at 7s.6d.

Kit's confidence in the project was based on the introduction of one-pound cheeses for domestic use and on his ability to turn whey, a waste product, into cash by transporting it in a tanker to a piggery in Widdale. He bought the pigs on credit. When they were fattened up for market, he gave the seller the option of re-purchasing them. Kit was to write: "As a pig will drink from three to four gallons of whey each day it has become a great friend of the factory dairy-man because of its help in disposing of what might otherwise be a very unpopular by-product." The first year's activity yielded a profit of £1,495.

When, in 1936, Bob Calvert was married, his big brother Kit presented him with the farm and, hence-forth, concentrated on making cheese. By 1937, a second delivery van was operating. It had been bought second-hand, as the name *Wilkinson's Pomfret Cakes* on its sides proclaimed. Kit passed his driving test. The van's rounds extended from Penrith and Keswick to Nelson and Burnley. In summer, which was espe-cially hot, the vehicle belonging to Johnny Hunter, the Stockton cheese factor, had broken down. The fac-tor said he had plenty of cheese left. Kit drove to Stockton in his little 1926 Jowett two-seater and found about 8 cwt of out-of-condition cheese in a dis-used stable.

Kit had the cheese weighed and offered to give the man the equivalent in clean stock for collection when his van was operational. The cheese in the stable was conveyed to Norton Congregational Church by ragged boys using two handcarts – with the promise of sixpence each . Unsuccessful applicants for the job, who had arrived with barrows, even prams, were treated to sweets that Kit purchased at a corner shop. The minister of the Church, who was known to Kit, distributed the cheese among old men who attended a regular get-together meeting. One old chap took a cheese for a woman with six children and a husband who was out of work.

Before the 1939-45 war, Wensleydale cheese was made on over a hundred local farms. By 1945, only half a dozen farmhouse cheese-makers were left, none of them being in Wensleydale. High-moisture cheese had not fitted in with the rationing scheme. A good deal of its weight might be lost through evaporation. When the ration for an individual was 1 oz per head per week, such a contraction was irritating for a retailer who had received an exact weight of cheese.

Kit lived into the age when cheeses were being wrapped in polythene. He had reckoned "nowt" to such a practice, considering that cheese wrapped in the traditional linen bandage had a better flavour. Now he ruefully admitted that since polythene was introduced the sale of 1lb "baby" cheeses had rocketed. In 1953, Kit built a new creamery on a spacious site beside the road to Gayle. I visited him when the work was half-done. He was anxious to keep fit, for he was apportioning jobs on a daily basis. It was necessary to form a new company, Wensleydale Creameries Ltd., with a capital of £30,000.

The construction was undertaken by William Dinsdale, of Gayle, who said the work could be done for between £15,000 and £16,000, which was substantially lower than a price quoted by an architect who had not taken local craftsmen into account. The work was completed for £14,640. The directors, delighted at Mr Dinsdale's work, gave him £250 of shares in the new company.

Don Thompson, a deputy head at Little Horton, Bradford, remembers the homely manner with which Kit showed visitors the cheese-making processes. Kit himself greeted two coachloads of children, three to a seat, a hundred in all, at the entrance. In next-to-no time, they were being shown the curdling vats. Then Kit got a ladle and invited the children to sample the whey, later explaining how it was used to fatten pigs. "So on finally into the maturing room where he demonstrated how he sampled the 32lb cheeses. He then invited the children to gather round a table. They were about a dozen deep. He took down a 32lb cheese and, with his penknife began cutting off pieces and offering them to the children. In the end, all the cheese had gone."

Don and the Brigantes Rover Crew inaugurated the Dalesman Hike, which ended at Hag Dyke, a farmstead high on Great Whernside that was now being used by Scouts as a field centre. Those who completed the Hike were fed on regional food. "We had ordered three hundred Vale of Mowbray pork pies to go with a salad meal and we warmed up six hundred Chorley Cakes... Kit donated a couple of 32lb cheeses. These we distributed at the same time together with slices of rich fruit cake."

By the 1960s, production of the Baby Wensleydale, a 1 lb cheese that the average housewife might buy weekly, had risen to 250,000 a year. The Milk Marketing Board, recognising the potential, bought the creamery for £500,000 and persuaded Kit to continue to run it. Kit did not forget the dale's heritage of farmhouse cheese. He arranged that at the entrance to the creamery a butter-churn would be on view.

Kit retired from full-time association with the

creamery in 1967 but remained a director. In 1971, still operated by the Milk Marketing Board, it found employment for sixty people.

YORKSHIRE CHEESECAKE

At the farms of upper Wensleydale, wives took a particular pride in the making of cheesecakes, which Kit Calvert said was a special afternoon tea pastry. He was given a traditional recipe for Cheesecake by one of the Guy family of Muker and passed that recipe on to me.

Curd. Take one pint of warm milk and add the starter – half a teaspoonful of rennet. Let this stand for an hour, then cut the curd and drain in muslin until all the whey is out.

Filling. To each 6 oz of curd add 3 oz of sugar, 2 oz of currants, 4 oz of butter or margarine, nutmeg, a pinch of salt and one egg.

Method. Beat the curd until fine, then add sugar, fruit, nutmeg, egg and salt and, finally, the butter or margarine that had been softened to a cream. Have ready tins lined with short pastry and fill these with the mixture. Flavour with rum if desired.

BOOK-COLLECTOR

Comfortably retired, with money in the bank and his own 400-acre farm in Widdale, Kit said: "I have gathered as much of this world's goods as I need. I want a la'al bit o' time to myself now." He continued to be a man-about-town, buying himself a black and white pony called Dolly and a donkey he named Jack. Dolly was regularly harnessed to a governess trap on gala day when Kit drove the gala queen through the town to the sports field. The placid Dolly also hauled the trap for Santa Claus as he made a grand entry into Hawes on Saturdays prior to Christmas Day. Kit purchased an Irish jaunty cart. For a time, until he became unruly, Jack featured in donkey rides.

When the books written by James Herriot were adapted for the television screen, Dolly became a film star. I once saw Kit holding her as I crossed from Askrigg into Swaledale on a day when "shooting" was taking place. He pointed out the BBC version of a dalesman who had just asked Kit if he was "speaking all right". Said Kit: "He wasn't. But what could I say?" Kit loved his dialect. He said: "Standard English cannot give us the warmth of feeling and comradeship that we get from our native dialect."

Associated with his dialect was a love of the printed word. Kit, aged nine, had howled at his father – who throughout his life never owned a book – and demanded, of all things, a Collins clear-type dictionary, price one shilling. Father, though only a struggling quarryman, bought the book. His collecting mania was set off when he read a copy of Edmund Bogg's *Eden Vale to the Plains of York*. The author had cycled to Hawes with a pack of books for sale.

Kit's book-collecting became an obsession. "I enjoy every hour I handle my books but, as I say, they keep you poor." At a farm sale in Swaledale in about 1948 he saw a copy of *Ogilby's Book of Roads*, dated 1698. To acquire it, he had to buy over six hundredweight of books. He did not bother to bring the other volumes away. He had a run of copies of the *Wensleydale Advertiser*, which was edited by Fletcher Clarke. The newspaper appeared fortnightly, from 1844 to 1849, price 2½d a copy. Each copy bore a tax stamp.

On a visit to Lancaster, he asked the proprietor of a second-hand bookshop if he had any volumes about Yorkshire. "Don't know," was the reply, "but you can go into the attic: there's a pile of books up there." Kit returned home rejoicing, having bought – for sixpence – a copy of *Methodism in Swaledale*, by John Ward.

Kit would collect owt that took his fancy. He attended the sale following the death of R A Scott Macfie of Shaws, in 1935. The day was as wild as the funeral day had been pleasant. "It was ower cowd to snaw," Kit recalled. Tom Milner, of Hawes, the auctioneer, was not anxious to prolong the sale. There were bargains galore. For a grand piano, Tom started off hopefully asking for £100 but those present did not fancy having to move it from the remote house. Kit bought this and a smaller, equally notable family piano, for 31s. When the creamery lorry collected his purchases, the legs of the grand piano were removed and the instrument upended and taken to the lorry on rollers. (Kit's wife blanched when she saw the pianos; they had two already).

Kit's Bookshop, when I first knew it, was sparsely furnished. A small round table held a Bible, open at

Proverbs. A note informed a potential purchaser that if no-one was in attendance they should "contact Mr C Chapman, grocer, next door." Mr Chapman kept an old tin box for that purpose. Kit's bookshop is not in its original position – a shop beneath the office of Malcolm E Scott, solicitor. For over 25 years, from 1951, this single-room bookshop in the main street of Hawes was the talk of the town.

It was a cal-oil [gossiping place] on market day. About 5,000 books, set haphazardly on floor-to-ceiling shelves, were available at 10p for a hardback, 5p for a less substantial work. He remarked to one browser: "You can have anything at a bob [shilling]. If you don't think it's worth a bob, then give me a tanner [sixpence]." He loved all his books and if he could not find a specific title he seemed quite despondent, commenting: "I hope it hasn't been sold."

There was the obligatory musty smell to excite seekers after bargains. The absence of classification was part of the fun. A browser might use one of two rush-bottomed chairs, of curious design, which Kit had picked up at a sale for 50p. Kit and those of his friends who, on market day, had come to town and had some time to kill, occupied two other chairs near the door. One visitor, to whom Kit mentioned there was little demand for theological works and the stock was "a dead duck", turned out to be a bishop on holiday. An elderly lady shocked Kit by asking if he had any "blue" books for sale. She wanted books bound in blue that would tone with her blue curtains.

Among the first stock was the book collection of Stanley Umpleby, dialect expert, who died at Sedbusk in 1953. Annie Metcalfe, who revered books, offered to run the shop – for nothing. John Mason later "got it on a business footing". John had started work at Hawes as a lad porter. One of his duties, at 5-45am, had been to fill the foot-pans to warm up the compartments of the passenger trains. The job took an hour and a-half. The compartments were lit by paraffin, later with gas lamps. John Mason clambered on the carriage roofs, lifting small lids to ignite the gas.

The arrangement at the bookshop was that Kit would buy the books and John Mason would sell them and keep the ledgers. He described the shop as "Hawes University" and proclaimed himself as the bursar. Each evening, even in wild weather, he insisted on walking up to Kit's home to report on the day's sales. On several occasions the takings were a mere thruppence. John Mason died in 1975, aged 92. The bookshop now looked after itself. Kit's brother-in-law, who lived in the market place, opened the shop in the morning and locked up at night. He held the key – the only key.

At the centre of the room was a table, littered with leaflets and holding a chapel collection plate on to which a purchaser placed his or her money if – as often happened – the proprietor had just "popped out". (The plate was succeeded by an Oxo tin and then a burglar-proof box that was attached to the table by a six inch nail). Beside the table were the two rush-bottomed reclining chairs, of curious design. A Victorian letterbox (wall-type) occupied a corner into which it had been placed when the post office allowed it to be purchased for a Hawes Museum.

The bookshop was never intended to provide Kit with a living. "It's a hobby and a real gossip shop," he would say. Local people, observing how many of Kit's cronies dropped in for a chat, referred to the bookshop as the "House of Commons". A journalist who spent three hours here recorded that Kit had not sold any books but had given three away. "I always say that it if makes my bacca money and covers the cost of a drop or two of petrol, I'm satisfied," he told me.

In 1965, Kit presented his personal collection of about a thousand books about Yorkshire – a library valued at £3,000 – to the Wensleydale County Modern School at Leyburn; they were to be known as the Calvert Collection. Having disposed of the books, Kit then quietly set about re-stocking the empty shelves.

LAY PREACHER

He preeaches on t'ferst day o' t'week,
An' practices on awt' others.
An' all on uz, rich an' poor alike
To him are men an' brothers.
(F A Carter).

A devout Christian of the old type, Kit regarded the circumstances of his conversion as too sacred for general publication, adding that he was prepared to tell it to anyone upon private inquiry. He was deacon and secretary of Hawes Congregational chapel. The room at his bungalow that served as a study had a standard fireplace, on which reposed a bottle of communion wine that was taken periodically to the nearby chapel. His saddest moment came when the chapel was closed in 1982. He took practical steps to keep the Congregational chapel at Leyburn open, buying it and arranging for the services to be conducted by himself or one of his friends.

He was a preacher in the homely yet forceful Dales manner. His translation of passages from the Bible into the dialect of his native district was criticised by some, to whom Kit replied: "Christ spoke in a dialect." When Christ was born (as reported in St Luke's Gospel, chapter 2), his mother "lapped him in a barrie cooat an' laid him in a manger, fer ther' was neea room fer 'im I' t'ludgin' hoose." Then there was the story of Jesus coming across the disciples as they were fishing in Galilee (St John's Gospel, chapter 21). "He ca'ed oot tew 'em: 'Lads, hey ye caught owt?' Th' shooted back: 'Nowt'. Sooa He sez: 'Kest yer net ower t'reet side ev t'booat an' ye'll git a catch.'" They did as they were advised and "cudn't rive't back fer t'weet o'fish in't."

The Psalms made a strong appeal to this dale-header:

The Lord is my Shipperd
Ah'll want for nowt.
He lets m' bassock i' t'best pastur an taks m'
Bi' t'watter side whar o's wyet on peeceful.
He uplifts mi soul, an' maks things seea easy 'at
Ah can dew what's reet an' Glorify His neeame,
Even if ah git t'death deaursteead ahs nut bi freetened,

Fer he'll bi wi' mi,

His creuk an'esh plant 'll up hod mi,

Thoo puts a good meal afoor mi,

Reet anenst them 'at upbraids mi,

Thoo ceuls mi heead wi' oil,

Ah Ah've meeat an' drink t' spar'.

Seurlie Thi goodness an' mercy 'al bi mine

Fer o' t'days o' mi life

An ah'll beleng t' t'hoose o' the Lord fer ivver.

During the 1939-45 war, when a minister left Keld in Swaledale and there was no layman to take services at the chapel, Kit and the Hawes minister attended in turn so that the doors would be kept open on Sundays. The minister had a breakdown in health. Kit travelled to Keld on most Sundays during a long winter. Incidentally, Kit's fondness for motoring led him to attempt to break into the mass car market with the prototype Curlew two-stroke, front-wheel-drive car. The bizarre project had engine faults and was written off in 1947, after clocking up only twenty-five miles. For years, as a rusting relic, it lay in a barn and was used by roosting chickens.

It was a special joy to hear Kit read from his own

translation of passages from The Good Book, especially St John's gospel, chapter nineteen:

Than Pilate teuk Jesus an' had Him flogged. An' t'sowgers pletted thorn twigs intev a croon an' put it on His heead an' dressed Him up in a perple goown an' shooted, "Hail! King o' the Jews" and brayed him with ther fists. Than Pilate cam' oot yance maar an' sez tew 'em , "Leuk; what a Man!"

B't when t'chief preeasts an' ther lackeys saa Him, the' shooted, "Crucify Him Crucify Him!" Seea Pilate sez, "Than tak Him t'crucify, b't let it bi knaan 'at Ah finnd neea faat in Him."

B't t'Jews chuntered back, "We hev a law, an' bi oor law He sud dee, fer He mak's hizsel oot ta bi the Son o' God." When Pilate heeard that, he was maar flade ner ivver an' went back inta t'coortroom an' sez t' Jesus, "Now what' do ye co' frae?" But Jesus nivver let on.

Seea Pilate sez tev Him, "Wheea't ye speeak t' mi? Dooa't ye knaa 'at Ah hey pooer t' hev ye crucified; an Ah've pooer t' let ye off?"

"Ye hev neea pooer agen mi," sez Jesus, "nabbut what's bin geean t' ye fra aboon; but him 'at handed mi ower t' ye hez t'bigger sin laid agen him." Fra' than on Pilate did aw he cud t' let Him off, but t'Jews shooted, "If ye let this feller lowse yer neea friend o' Ceasar. Annibody 'at sets hizsel up t' bi a King is agan Ceasar."

When Pilate heeard that, he had Jesus browt ootside, an' sat hizsel doon ont' judgement steean in t'spot knaan as t'Peeavemint, er as t'Jews co'as it "Gabbatha".

An' th' war makken ready fer t'Passower Feeast; an' 'twas aboot dinner-time, an' he sez to t'Jews, "Leuk at yer King." But th' shooted back, "Away wi' Him! Crucify Him!" "Nay," sez Pilate, "wad ye hey mi crucify yer King?" "We have neea king, nobbut Ceasar," says t'chief preeasts.

At that he handed Jesus ower tev 'em t' bi crucified, an' off th' went wi' Him, an' meeade Him hug His Cross on t'rooad up tev a spot ca'd "The Skull", or ez t'Hebrews had yance neeamed it "Golgotha", an' thar th' crucified Him an' other tweea, yan at ayther side, an' Jesus on t'middle cross.

An' Pilate wreeate a nooatice an' had it fastened on t'middle cross, an' t'wordin' was: "Jesus fra Nazareth. King o' the Jews."

CHAPEL TALES

Kit's upbringing was in a world made up of the good and the bad, of moral issues that were a contrasting black and white, with no shades of grey. Most of the people had religious affinities, church or chapel, with chapels of various denominations in the numerical ascendancy. "There was a social division," said Kit. "The church people were the professionals, landowners, bankers and such like. Ordinary working people were Nonconformists." In Wensleydale, a sprinkling of Meeting Houses, raised by Quakers, were far more venerable than the Wesley chapels. Those who built little wayside chapels in remote areas were sometimes confronted by heaps of stone. Farmers owning horses and carts transported them from quarry or beck-bottom for this purpose.

The period Kit Calvert recalled was one of chapels brimming over with worshippers and of local preachers who, speaking passionately, in everyday language, stoked up fears, confirmed hopes and maintained a "hot line" to the Almighty. The preacher charged his prayers with high emotion. Kit told of one man who had tears running down his face as, with hands together, he conversed with his mother. She had "gone to her reward" years before. "Ay, mother," he would declare, "you can see I've been faithful." Gayle, the chapel he attended, was noted for the frequency of shouted Hallelujahs, coupled with "praise the Lord" and "save 'em."

Kit related a case of level-pegging. The parish church at Hawes had been built "in t'same year they built Bethel. Eighteen fifty one. There must have been a great religious movement then." Religious differences were evident in the Smith family, owners of a woollen mill. They were "church people" until James, one of two brothers, became a Nonconformist. He pressed his brother to sell a piece of ground at the end of Springbank, where they lived, so a manse and Congregational chapel could be built. The brother, a devout Anglican, insisted on a provision that trees should be planted to hide the new manse from Springbank. The trees were close-set and when they reached maturity were like an immense barrier, "so much so that if you looked out of t'manse you couldn't see down to t'road."

A local preacher was prepared to walk, cycle or go on horseback to remote chapels. Such a man was Old Jack Harrison. His eyes stuck out like the proverbial chapel hat-pegs when his son-in-law, who was also a preacher, turned up at his house in the 1930s with a new car, the seating of which was "as comfy as cushions." Jack related that "when we set off, it was like sitting in an armchair. I thought about t'owd days when I used to walk for miles. Or travel on horseback on a cold, wild neet. There were so much clatter and talk I couldn't think of a Message, not even when I'd been dropped off at the bridge in Hawes and t'driver went on to Gayle." Jack, standing in the vestry at Hawes chapel, thought to himself: "This is a job. I'se here. And no Message." He clambered into the pulpit, looked around and "sees Owd Moss [Kit's father] who'd told me o' Tuesday he was coming to hear me. What should I do? I just clasped me hands together an' shut mi' eyes and I says: 'Lord – give us a Message, if it's only for Owd Moss.' Did he let me down? No. I preached for half an hour and five minutes – and nivver got me tale hawf finished."

Kit said that Jack "had some good Truths that were

given in a quaint way. Kit entered into the spirit of the time when he recalled Old Jack's rendering of the story of the Prodigal Son. Jack declared, in a voice of such power it rattled the windows: "It says in t'Good Book he would fain hev filled his belly with the husks the swine did eat. But he didn't. D'ye knaw why he didn't? Now 'es any of you ever bin hungry? I have. Have you ever been that hungry you'd eat pig-meat? I have. But I was never as hungry as that lad was. Why did he leave t'husks alone? Or feed issen on pig-meat? He had a godly fadder. And I believe he had a godly mother. He'd been taught what was his own and what was other folks's. That pig-meat wasn't his. When he'd left home, he got what his fadder had gi'n him. It was his own. He spent it. He wasted it. But it was his own. He could do what he liked wi' it – till he had nowt. There was pig-meat. But he couldn't eat it. He'd been taught what were reight and what were wrang. If he'd ate it – it'd hev choked him!"

For the Prodigal, this was the turning point. He would go home. Jack ended his sermon by declaring: "That lad was better off than a lot today. A godly home means a lot!"

The Message was the thing. One year, when Kit

had "spent missen on two Harvest Festival addresses", he discovered he was due to preside at Bainbridge – and the speaker "couldn't come – he'd got laryngitis and had lost his voice. So I went up to Gayle to see if I could get one of them lads to help ma. No. They couldn't. They hadn't an address ready. I called at Old Tom's, who lived a fair way down t'dale. He said he would have helped if he hadn't been taking t'harvest festival service at Walden. So that put paid to Tom." In the end, it was creaky-legged Old Jack who agreed to give the address. Said Kit: "It's more than likely he did not know what he was going to say as he climbed the pulpit steps."

Missions were conducted by visiting evangelists. Sometimes their words fell "on stony ground". At Gayle chapel about 1930, said Kit, two simple-minded women preached in the old Methodist style. "They told the old story. Their illustrations were vivid. A farmer who received an invitation to one of the meetings scoffed at them, then rode his horse home. The horse shied at something at the roadside. The farmer fell off and broke his neck. He was found dead. Well, the way they played on that. They had 'em all freightened to death." The witness of the two ladies at Gayle transformed the lives of half a dozen young men, who eventually served as local preachers. One, James Alderson, became a Methodist minister.

At a camp meeting, held annually, the "loving cup", filled with water, was passed round and each person sipped from it. There were two main speakers but anyone could break in and testify to the Love of God. Kit was sad to observe how this event had changed until it was like an anniversary "rather than the passionate camp meeting that it used to be." One of those attending was Richard Alderson, who was – said Kit – almost a mystic. He was once inspired to intercept two evangelists who, having achieved nothing at Hawes, were on their way to Sedbergh. Richard, presuming the Devil had been intervening, prayed aloud that the Lord should "tak him away". He added: "I should have been shepherding, but the Lord sent me across here to stop you. Go back – and you'll have some converts tonight." They came back and carried on for three weeks. They increased the roll of members in Hawes chapel by over eighty.

Kit was persuaded that religious loyalties were diluted through wartime experiences. He was thinking of the Great War. "A lot of young people, good people, mixed up in the maelstrom of the War, saw a wider world and upsetting experiences. When they came back from War, they were different people. Older people who had not been to the war carried on in the old ways – till they died off." The Methodism that had been the core of the social life of the Dales was toned down when those who felt a call to preach were faced with oral and written examinations.

In the days of heartfelt Dales religion, a chapelgoer was going to feed some cattle one morning when he had to pass another cow-byre, from which came an unusual noise. Kit related that it came from an old lay preacher who, standing in the hay-mew, was praying mightily for a lad who was breaking the hearts of his parents through his wild ways. "Within a fortnight, that wild lad was at the penitent form at Gayle chapel. He became a member and a class leader." The old man himself had not known his prayers were being overheard.

As Kit said: "Nowt like that happens today."

LAST DAYS

When Kit bought Springbank at Hawes he also acquired an acre of land in front of the house where he realised an old ambition – to provide local children with a playground. The Army during the 1939-45 war commandeered the ground. Nine large Nissen huts were erected here. When in due course they were demolished, the concrete bases remained. They became the nucleus for the playground.

The swings, a roundabout and slide, also a number of seats, were paid for out of the Army compensation. The Army officer who negotiated a settlement of £1,200 was permitted to allow a figure not exceeding £400. So Kit accepted £399.10s – and, with a shrug, reconciled himself to paying the difference. He had a prolonged disagreement with the planning authority. When they said they would send him a plan, Kit had remarked that he would burn it. When, in due course, the playground was opened, the planning officer spoke cordially about the scheme.

The playground endures to remind the folk of Hawes of Kit's benevolence.

On July 11, 1975, Kit's wife died. They had been married for forty-four years. In February, 1977, Kit was in Buckingham Palace, receiving the MBE from the Queen Mother. He had been honoured during the Queen's Jubilee year. He died in January, 1984, aged 80. Kit had commented: "If I ever leave Hawes, it will be in a box."

At the funeral service, Kit's old friend, the Rev James Alderson, said: "Many local families owe their jobs to his tenacious fighting qualities. The parish was saved from being a ghost town and just a haunt for holidaymakers."

Kit's dying wish was honoured when Dolly, the pony, now nineteen years of age, was harnessed to the cart on which the coffin reposed. When, next, his granddaughter saddled up the pony for a ride, Dolly led her to the cemetery, walked through the open gate and stood beside Kit's grave.

UPDATE

In May, 1992, a subsidiary of the Milk Marketing Board named Dairy Crest closed the creamery and transferred production of Wensleydale cheese to – Lancashire! The ex-managers took up the fight and, against the odds, persuaded the owners to sell them the creamery. A management buy-out was agreed in November, 1992. In the following month, some of the former workforce recommenced the making of cheese. They had a goodly amount available for sale at Christmas.

A drawing of Kit's head, plus battered trilby and clay pipe, appears on promotional material. Kit is associated by name with the dairy's 200g and 500g cheeses, the larger cheese being wrapped in muslin cloth, as the old chap preferred. Kit would have been startled but impressed by the varieties produced to meet changing times and varying tastes. Wensleydale cheese is available with cranberries or onions and chives; with apricots or stem ginger. The 200g

Coverdale is an original cheese from the dale, re-introduced and finished in black wax.

Another product that Kit would have applauded was Wensleydale made from ewe's milk, harking back to the old monastic days and much appreciated by those who are allergic to the milk of cows. Also available is traditional Wensleydale cheese naturally "cold-smoked" over oak and hardwood chips.

Kit's Bookshop endures in an alley close to the original place. The owner, sensitive to Kit's aspirations, helps to keep alive the memory of a notable dalesman.

Kit is an ordinary man, loyal to God and with a love for his fellow men.

(James Alderson, a former school friend).

I suppose Kit Calvert can be thought of as just another awkward old Yorkshireman… but to me he's a bit of a hero.

(Don Mosey, author and broadcaster).

His interests were many… above all, his love of Wensleydale and its people.

(Brochure produced by Wensleydale Creamery at Hawes).